Burnt Fields Under Snow

Burnt Fields Under Snow

Poems by

R.G. Pagano

Cover design by Shay Culligan
Cover image by Nancy Deveno
Author photo by R.G. Pagano

ISBN: 979-8-90146-901-9
Library of Congress Control Number: 2026931924

Kelsay Books
502 South 1040 East, A-119
American Fork, Utah 84003
Kelsaybooks.com

For Nancy

Acknowledgments

In memory of my cousin, dottoressa Anna Di Paolo, and her mother and my great-aunt, Filomena Pagano, for introducing me to Italy and my heritage, an immersion that had me dreaming in Italian during my stay in their Atripalda home. To my good friend Giovanni Sponza, many thanks for providing my writing place, a kind of writer-in-residence program in Bassano del Grappa, Italy. To Judith Perry McCaffrey and Toby Hubbard, *mille grazie* for editorial guidance on my early drafts.

To the editors of the following publications that first presented poems in this collection, thank you for your encouragement:

Harrow House Journal: "Whenever You Think of Me"

Ho Girato il Mondo per Incontrarti: "Among the Ice Crystals"

Nei Miei Occhi, Tu: "Whenever You Think of Me"

(The two Italian anthologies listed above are associated with the Premio San Valentino—Atripalda, Italy.)

Contents

I.

At 90 mph

145 km/h

On a quiet Sunday morning
where Sabino was waiting,
I arrived on a charter flight
to Rome in the summer of 1985.

I liked it that way:
the sleepy airport at Ciampino,
the dry heat,
that it was Sunday.

My cousin introduced himself;
then we headed south
in his Alfa Romeo at 90 mph
along the way to Atripalda.

Atripalda

Roman ruins decay near a farmhouse.

Those ruins are the remains of homes
with pools and courtyards and mosaic floors,
with walls of circle and flower designs in Pompeii pink
from a time when Atripalda was Abellinum
and the Saturday River moved goods to ancient towns.

The Romans conquered Abellinum,
building aqueducts and baths and an amphitheater
before abandoning them during the Greek-Gothic wars.

On the other side of the Saturday River,
near the church of Sant'Ippolisto,
a reawakening would follow.

The church of Sant'Ippolisto has its own crypt
with early Christian bones in cases of glass and bronze
in a chapel with frescoes on ceilings and walls,
and beyond the chapel,
other frescoes of angels holding flags, staffs, and flowers.

Sant'Ippolisto was the parish of my great grandfather,
who after his first son died
in the Great War on Monte Grappa,
sent his second born, my grandfather, to America.

Monte Grappa

On this mountain
covered in snow
from the night before,
I found my great-uncle's tomb
on Cima Grappa
in white fog
hiding the panorama
from the names of the fallen.

I could never pretend to understand
how bad it was,
how important after the defeat at Caporetto, or
what might have gone through his mind,
the flashes of life experiences before he died,
why his mother awoke and
knew her son would not be coming home.

The massif of Grappa rises
from the great plains of Veneto
between the Brenta and Piave rivers,
under the eyes of the Virgin Mary
who I imagine cried when the Great War
reached Monte Grappa.

Below Cima Grappa, a footbridge crosses a canyon
joining the Valle di Santa Felicita.

A convoy moves supplies to the front,
passing stone markers alongside a road.
The road turns into a horseshoe
inside Monte Caston where artillery builds a death spiral.

Shells grow into their own piles of ant hills.

In trenches, fortified by
stones, sandbags, and wood and barbed wire on top,
soldiers dig in after a pause.

One soldier peers over the rocks with his binoculars.

The front lines extend through the mountain range to forge a river,
whose red current kills after being flooded by the flamethrowers
shooting black smoke and fire into the sky.

On the other side of the mountain,
the wounded wait for the next ambulance.

I imagine the faithful seeing an apparition.
They know the Virgin Mary would never leave them.
Perhaps my great-uncle was among them,
and during a rush of images that filled his mind,
felt Her warmth lifting his spirit
as he shed the artillery, the pain and fear
until his thoughts swept
at once and forever into the light
before understanding why.

Among the Ice Crystals

Snow fell,
silence followed
for a couple
to create their life
together.

Like scouts
exploring ruins,
ancient mysteries,
to rediscover
what had been lost,
their love
from another time.

Old souls
whose hearts beat as one
in their refuge,
where time

e

v a p

o

r a t e s

among the ice crystals
keeping the noise

at

bay.

Permit to Stay

The cover of my passport was peeling from its back,
but I surrendered it and Nancy's; then waited
with the patience of melting wax facing a kind of altar
until our names were called by the Questura,
police headquarters in Vicenza.

I used an old bank reference.
Nancy had a sabbatical letter, a receipt of half salary
although the letter omitted any amount.
A bank letter is what the Questura wanted,
a receipt of real money, which I pulled out,
showing the amount we had just moved into
our new Lira account.

Later that day, each of us signed the
Permesso di Soggiorno per Stranieri,
pleased to have received a year to stay in Italy.

Giovanni's House

Paintings often describe a place,
and it was no different for us
when Nancy rendered her impressions
of where we lived in Italy:
a house and its gardens,
the fields alongside,
bug and tin collections.
Objects in our flat sat
as she transformed them
into shapes defined by colors on canvas.

During those first months
and with great interest,
Nancy painted her interpretation
of our residence
that had been in Giovanni's family
for three generations.

Topolino

On the other side of a wall
covered in vines over terracotta slats,
a *pappagallo* captured our attention.
The parrot's army hymn was curious,
a kind of Alpine rendition of
some melodic song from World War One.

Winter arrived.

We expected to hear the hymn
from inside our neighbor's apartment
on the lesser side of the house;
instead, only faint sounds of birds emerged.
I began to think that the birds were not part of the extended family
but holed up in the space between our ceiling and the roof.
We never saw the birds,
the way we never saw the woodworms,
except for their handiwork,
the bottom of dressers sawed away
and piles of sawdust on the pine floor.

About that time, my wife dreamt of a past life,
which made us wonder about the history
of the people who had lived here in Italy
and whether the sounds were the rattling of spirits.
The Bassano house was built in 1850 for an estate owner,
and during the Second World War, each room sheltered a family.

We never saw

m i s t   c r a w l i n g

around our flat
or anything that looked or acted like a spirit.

It was not my grandfather's house in upstate New York.
The 8mm film of him and his dog Duke
near the entrance of the property by an oak tree
runs through my mind whenever I think about him.
He died in a corner room off the living room,
where I slept a decade later as a teenager visiting my uncle.
I believed my uncle when he told me
about the white mist floating in the middle of the night.
The piano playing, vacuum cleaning, and doorbell ringing
all conspired to heighten the angst.
None of the sounds could be explained, he insisted,
especially after disconnecting the wires from the doorbell.

The *pappagallo's* hymn,
the dull sounds, and
our talk of spirits

f
 a d
   e
d.

Then we saw this baby mouse,
a *topolino* darting across the pine floor under the archway
separating the kitchen from the dining area.
Without my glasses, it was a blur
but not a spirit kind of blur.

When I told the landlord,
he carried his cat Dante up to our flat;
after removing a strip of wood at the base of the kitchen cabinet
and opening the door under the sink,
he left him to control the *topolino.*

Dante moved inside the cabinet
near the *bombola* that fires the stove,
hunkering down like a statue except for his tail.

This state of play was unfamiliar, I thought.
Often Dante would climb two flights of stairs,
and between the steps and door to our apartment,
jump and open the door while landing on his paws.

Then visit.

More than an hour had passed before hearing a scuffle.

Seeing the *topolino* in Dante's mouth
jolted my perception to render something less real,
like an animation or some augmented reality gone awry.

Release and chase led to a

f
r
e
e
f
a
l
l

through the middle of the staircase,
conjuring up notions of reincarnation,
a spirit not moving in a mist but through Dante.

After the chase moved outside into the snow,
the army hymn replayed in my mind.
The illusion of hearing the *pappagallo* lasted only seconds,
which was ample time to miss the end
and hope that the *topolino* was able to escape.

Is Gedi with You?

"Why are you bothering me?" The cow seemed to say.
"We're looking for peace," I thought to answer.
"Here?"
"Yes here."
"Is Gedi with you?"

The cow didn't mind a Belgian Sheepdog
who had befriended him some days ago.
Gedi was that way, not so much to make friends,
but to amuse himself with the cats at home,
mostly Dante,
and with the ducks, despite their reluctance
to engage in activities that had
little to do with eating grass and feed,
drinking water and bathing,
and cleaning themselves
when they are not flapping their wings.

Gedi had mimicked the cow,
stepping close and looking up
before pulling back and stopping;
then waiting for the cow to mime Gedi
until they danced to barks.

Gedi could tell me what the cow was thinking, I thought,
if the cow was thinking, which he seemed to be,
at least more than the ducks.

"Gedi's home," I finally said. "*Non c'è qui.*"

The cow peered through the fence
looking for his shepherd friend.

II.

Of Course I Stopped

Bastia Hill

The black vines filled the greens,
which rolled across the landscape
and around the yellow and gold trees
and the shadows they formed to the east.
Lines of poplar trees bordered cornfields
on flat land between the hills.

In the distance, silk leaves shimmered blue and green
in the late afternoon light on olive trees,
climbing other hills towards the Prealps
covered in pines and reaching up into the sky.

Larks flew overhead.
We could hear their songs
out of the Valle di Santa Felicita
in this vast extension of plains,
in this land that Dante Alighieri described
in his songs of paradise.

A lone tower stood on Bastia Hill,
Dante's tower.
It was a bell tower from an old church
built over the foundation of a castle,
il castello di Romano,
birthplace of Ezzelino III da Romano,
son of an imperial vicar and
grandson of a principal leader of the Second Crusade.

Two larks passed us.
I followed their flight

into a garden of red flowers,
fraught with pleasant fragrances.
On their way out, the larks
nearly found themselves in a net.

A hawk soared above,
extending its wings in a graceful flight.
Hang gliders circled mountain peaks
and pretended to be hawks
when there was enough wind.

I read that young Ezzelino hunted here,
that he learned from a falconer,
to catch

larks,

magpies,

partridges,

starlings.

What captivated Ezzelino?

The falcon resting on his fist?
Flying after its prey?

Heading for a lark,
with Ezzelino on horseback
as if he were the falcon
to seize the lark and
to bring it down like a falcon?

Why become a f
a
l
c
o
n,
and not a lark?

A tyger, not a lamb?

A tyrant?

Dante imprisoned Ezzelino
in his *Inferno,*
in a boiling river of blood
haunted by Centaur archers.

I was lost for a moment
until I saw men picking olives
in the orange glow of the sunset.

September 11

Away from the shed
in the middle of the garden,
smaller pines thrive
over larger plants and bushes and vegetation
containing yellow and orange flowers.
White palms break up the green view,
and through a fence
draped with leafy vines,
a line of vineyards intrudes.

"I started to paint the garden on the day
the Twin Towers were attacked," Nancy said.
"Of course I stopped."

Letter Writing

November 4, 2001

Marco,

A month after arriving,
I read the "Italian Survey" in *The Economist,*
which you gave us sometime before we left.
I had wanted to read it much sooner,
but packing and breaking down the apartment,
exhaustion on our Swissair flight,
then settling in our new flat
and obtaining permits to stay in Italy
kept getting in the way.

G8 in Genoa,
erupting only days after we arrived
was buried with many other news accounts
after September 11th.

We live simply here in Italy, without a TV or car,
and when we heard about the terrorist attacks in the States,
went into town on bicycle to a café with a TV.
The images were difficult to digest
and the distance from here to Massachusetts
aggravated our disconnect.

Not until Nancy and I
read accounts in *The New York Times*

did we feel closer
to what our fellow Americans
had felt and are still feeling.

People tell us that America has changed,
that Americans are more patriotic, united, and caring;
but also afraid of anthrax and more attacks
and are anxious and nervous.

Italians have been mostly sympathetic.

I apologize for not responding till now,
but I do practically no letter writing
when I am writing about our experiences,
threading the past into the present.

They are about us, why we love Italy,
where we live and the animals.

They are about rail travel, a wedding,
September 11th and understanding why.

Nancy paints
objects in our flat,
views from her studio
looking out towards cornfields,

outside and in the garden,
several of the house,
of plants and bushes and pines,
and more recently,
14th- and 17th-century villas
not far from where we live.

A presto.

—R

Homo Sapiens

We had become part of
the Venice Biennale,
pulled into dark rooms and
falling into black holes
unable to see until the videos started,
shedding light on
Alexander Roitburd's remake of
Ejzenstejn's *The Battleship Potëmkin,*
showing the same violence
mixing the original with modern images and
repeating them.

Without Care

In the deep indigo of space,
Earth reveals itself as a sanctuary
with blue green hues that welcome.
Amid the deafening silence,
tranquility glows there
like a beacon.

Below the clouds,
the quiet slips
into a stream of activity,
which at night glistens
and moves, bending light together
like a dance.

On the planet,
the flow begins to break down,
disrupting what our hearts seek,
a way of happiness,
and without care, with broken hearts,
we only see what is not there
like a mirage.

Padre Pio

In Pietrelcina, in southern Italy,
Francesco Forgione was born on May 25, 1887.
It was there he had his first visions of
angels and saints and demons.

In New York City, in Lower Manhattan,
terrorists cut the World Trade Center on September 11, 2001,
causing the steel columns to

m e l t,   the columns to

s e p a r a t e   and buckle, the floors to

e x p l o d e   and fall on the ones below

until the 110 stories of light glass-and-steel became rubble
inside of smoke and white ash and plaster dust.
The earth stood still that day.

This suffering tells us something.
It stops the forward-moving illusion we see,
stripping its layers and putting us in a kind of desert.

Francesco entered the convent of Morcone
to begin his initiation, where he became Fra Pio.
His health was frail, and in the mountains, worsened.

From the window of the other skyscrapers and lesser buildings,
from the other side of the Brooklyn Bridge
and across the Hudson River,
New Yorkers, we were all New Yorkers that day,
looked on as balls of fire exploded out of the towers,
one and then the other, exposing the demon
before vanishing behind plumes of gray and black smoke.

The revelation comes in moments that do not last,
but whose truth lingers

like a detour to another road,

and if we care to look, shows another way
before we reach a familiar crossroad,
and if we care to remember, moves us to

take that other road long after the detour comes down.

After being ordained as Padre Pio,
after seeing Jesus and the Virgin Mary in Piana Romana,
he saw red in the middle of his palms
and felt pain on the bottom of his feet.

People were throwing themselves from the towers;
others, covered with soot and blood, were

wondering why they were
among the dead,
among the twisted rubble of concrete and steel.

Padre Pio was called The Saint with the Stigmata.
He had the scent of violet and rose
that radiated from the blood of his wounds.

His spirit moved through time and space to comfort the dying.

Padre Pio, like Francesco d'Assisi,
experienced the suffering that Jesus endured on the cross.

Does going through this kind of suffering
take us somewhere beyond the violets and roses,
like Padre Pio who died leaving
not a trace on his hands or feet or ribs
after bearing the stigmata for 50 years?

Do we go where we think,
not alone but with guides like Padre Pio?
Perhaps he was there on September 11th
for the thousands who died,
to lift their souls from the weight of the rubble,
wrapping them in a warm light and
freeing them from the illusion that they had been forsaken.

REM

If my thoughts could take me to a place,
they could move me to a condition.

So, I thought of tranquility and
found myself in a chapel
surrounded by a forest.

Light beamed rays through stained glass.

Outside, the green felt good against the blue
where mourning doves carried their music inside,
lighting a candle and creating a silence that

put me in a flow.

Whenever You Think of Me

Do not grieve my love.
I am with you now,
whenever you think of me.

Feel my presence

not in the way we were
like love birds and their songs
in a world of pure joy,

but in the way we are
still together with each memory
even if you cannot see me.

Find me

in places that are sacred to us,
especially by the sea,
where we talked about our dreams,
listened to the waves, its whispers,
and if we lingered,
watched the orange glow of the sunset.
Don't you feel my embrace?

Be brave.

Do not cry. Smile.
Your smile is so beautiful.
It makes me want to smile. You know that.

Do you see the cardinal? Look!
There's another one, two love birds
with a

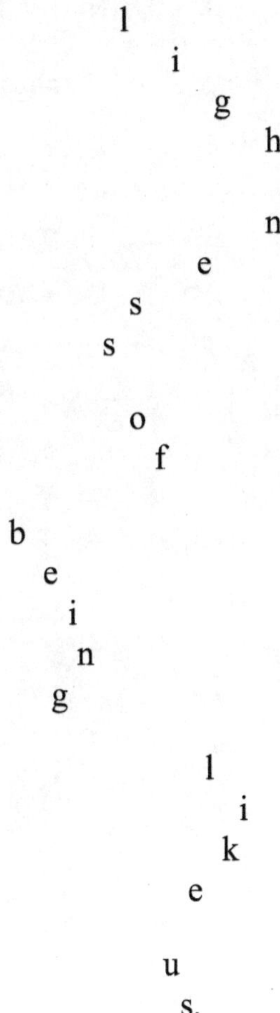

III.

As You Come Up for Air

Brenta River

The rippling rhythm
befriended us
inviting us
into its flow.

We hiked that morning,
beyond the timber bridge
by the river bank.

The water began to clap,
and around the bend,
swirl and drizzle in a mist
to the beat of a drum.

We danced to the tempo
bathing in the moment.

In step with the falling water,
the drummer infused the cascade
with his steadfast rapping
calling forth a kind of chanting
with veiled figures in procession.

We moved onward
deeper into the flow
of the Brenta River.

Writer's Block

I paused for a moment to question myself,
not the way they do in *Corriere della Sera* interviews
with heads of state and officials or experts on current events,
but on writing which is what I do in Italy
when I am not visiting museums or galleries with Nancy.

My initial thought was to ask about my handwriting,
more than once described as hieroglyphics;
then build the remaining questions organically.

What about hieroglyphics?

My handwriting was far worse
after being perfectly legible until high school
when someone stole my history notebook.
I vowed to make future notes worthless to anyone but me,
and took them in Spanish when I could
but mostly in my own lingo, a kind of hieroglyphics,
which I had difficulty reading when it was still in flux.
I truncated and combined letters;
then slanted them as if I were left-handed.

Are you left-handed?

I never held the pen properly,
not inside two fingers and my thumb
but sliding down four stuck together
like a mass leaning into the paper,
the thumb in the same place
saving the pen from falling.

Some years ago,
I spent time trying to write with my left hand.
I had no problem holding the pen correctly,
and the results were easier to read.
The experiment failed in the end because I was too slow.

My younger sister
remembers our elementary teacher
insisting that she use her right hand.

Are you handwriting stories?

All of my stories are in longhand.
There is a flow that goes on
when you draw across the paper.
I feel closer to the writing.
It slows the writing,
which causes me
to contemplate and
then come back to it.

Do you use an outline?

I simply write
while living in Italy
because even a year is brief.
I write impressions
while they are fresh
and those from the past
that connect and seem as current.

It is quiet where we live,
here on the edge of Bassano del Grappa.
For me, the setting is ideal for writing.

How would you describe your writing?

Lyrical. Vivid.
Reading a painting
but not seeing the words
at the same time
they are creating
the images in the mind's eye.

Perhaps it's the popular music in the background.
In one sense, I do not hear the Italian lyrics,
only sounds that work together to produce the harmony.
And some of it is so moving
that it enters my writing
the way long distance swimmers
glide through the water after the adrenaline kicks in.
It puts you into another world,
you feel that you can fly,
you start hearing the rhythm in your head
as you come up for air.

Where is the conflict?

Nancy works with color to define shapes on canvas.
It is not about the shapes, but how they are created using color.

My writing meanders.
The conflict if it exists is subtle,
sometimes elusive.

I hope there is
a connection to
something better,
something that inspires,
something beautiful.

What are your themes?

Since there is no outline,
I wonder if I'll know what to write next.
My stories describe past visits to Italy.
They are about the animals here.
They reference local folklore
and heaven and hell
in the hills not far from where we live.

What about writer's block?

At about the time Nancy was preparing for her art show,
I put my writing aside and started to work out ideas for a brochure.
I no longer thought about writing.

Then Nancy suggested writing a bicycle story,
and after we saw a man bicycling while talking on his cellphone,
I warmed up to the idea and began writing again.

Chimneys

A view outside her studio
was one of the first paintings
that Nancy completed.

"I had done a little painting
of an iron railing in front of a window.
I saw this view on the side of our neighbor's house
and wanted to show what was beyond the ironwork."

The blank side of a nondescript house
with its roof pointing upward at a 45-degree angle
and then falling
was beyond the railing
where you could see chimneys,
broken terracotta tiles,
and a glimmer of the landscape.

"Your eyes look at that,
the building that obstructs the view.
The viewer wants to see the landscape
and what it looks like.
It creates mystery."

39 Paintings

It took me two weeks to frame 39 paintings.

In a small garage on a workbench
with a miter box and saw,
I measured the sides of wood strips;
then cut the strips
and sanded the ends to bevel the joints.
The Fully Synthetic Mobil Oil
had nothing to do with the effort,
but I left it on the bench anyway.
Most of the paintings were small,
and the corners of the larger ones fit at the end of the workbench
without having to move the Lambretta 50 motor scooter.

Outside the garage at a wood table made from a fallen tree,
I nailed the wood strips to the sides of the canvas.
At first, I was slow to put the nails in straight.

When I paused,

I could hear the birds.
That was better than listening to the bee in the garage
by the ceiling fluorescent, which had its own kind of buzz.
At least the bee kept me company
not like the ducks who never bothered to look inside.

Gedi sometimes rested under the table as I

buried the nails with a
heavy hammer and
swift movements
to put them in straight.

He never complained about the pounding.

The last part of the framing process
involved nailing a triangle hook on the back of the strip
without causing the painting to

t
i
l
t

when hung.

Setting the triangle exactly in the middle
often failed to achieve this equilibrium.

So, I came up with another approach,
holding up the painting with my pencil
inside of the stretcher bar
until I could find the right balance
to level the bottom of the painting on the table.

My proficiency improved each time a frame was completed.
At the end, I became so good that the corners were almost perfect although I was less confident the triangle would hold the balance.

Between Color and Form

Shapes separated by color,
impressions on canvas paintings.

An armchair in a room.

Vines.

A train traveling through the plains,
away from the hills and bad weather.

Burnt fields under snow.

A cobalt sky of falling grain
whose horizon is broken by two cypress trees.

A wire between poles.

A hazy sky. A temple and three statues.

The interior of a café. A chandelier.

Umbrella trees, and in the distance,
a panorama of mountains after a rain,
silent except for
the ghosts of men hung for
resisting those who would occupy their spirit.

Yellow newspapers covering store windows.

White flowers in a vase next to furs.

A covered bridge and
its reflection in the Brenta River.

Cornfields, metal sheds and clothing on a line,
and below near the greenhouse, the garden.

Statuettes,
little Madonnas,
one from Lourdes,
on top of a tin with a green elephant,
along with
Arlecchino and Pulcinella.

White Umbrellas

White umbrellas over lounge chairs in beige sand
formed lines parallel to the shore,
not so deep ahead of the dunes and pine trees behind us.
In early July, the Adriatic Sea was calm.
Metal blue waves broke against a wall of rocks.
Far from the shore, sailboats emerged and held their positions
below low-hanging clouds pasted into the Lignano Riviera sky.

It was a nice way to end our year in Italy,
relaxing by the seashore in the early mornings and late afternoons
when the sun is sleepy,
and in between, bicycling everywhere else on the peninsula,
north to Lignano Pineta and Sabbiadoro and
south beyond the zoo to the other side of the river
to lettuce fields and greenhouse tomato plants not yet ripe.

"The colors are working," Nancy said.

Nancy filled the paper with yellow,
a bright strip around the edge
to frame the softer tones
against the trees bending with the wind
she could not paint the way she could paint the sky,
and in the distance, shrubs.
I liked the trees,
the nine of them together.

Nancy had water in a cup
next to her watercolor paints
and five brushes.

"The trick is to keep your colors looking fresh.
It's difficult. All color turns to gray,
not bad if you're doing gray paintings."

Where did all the sailboats go? I thought.

Coca Hotel

We found a hotel
close to Marco Polo Airport
on our last day in Italy,
and after checking in,
went off to Venice.

In the Chiesa del San Rocco,
Nancy took a pinhole photograph
with a camera she had made from a small cardboard box.
I recall when she painted the inside of the box black and
attached an elastic across the top to hold the film in place;
then used a pin to bore a hole to create the lens.
Previous black-and-white results were
wide views of frescoes on church ceilings and statues
along walls and pews and candles and flowers and marble floors,
not of any passerby, or Liza Minnelli in Taormina.

Giovanni had seen us off that morning,
taking us and our pieces of luggage to the train station in Bassano.
It was nice to stop for cappuccino under the vines near the station.
Not what Hemingway did in Venice somewhere in Dorsoduro
in whatever restaurant we walked into months ago, where
Nancy met an elderly woman who had waited on Hemingway
outside in the back in the garden under the vines.

What could we say?

We were just leaving for a time,
now standing on the train in the space between carriages
because it worked for our luggage and talking to Giovanni
who was smart to stay on the platform.

"Have you seen the *topolino?*" Giovanni asked.

Giovanni stretched and played
the part of a mouse reclining in a lounge chair
sponging the sun for rays on holiday
away from the work of
looking for food under our sink and
hiding from Dante or Bubù or any of the other cats.

The doors closed.
Giovanni stood there as the train took us away
from Bassano and the pre-Dolomites and Monte Grappa
under the clouds,
not like the Alps we passed on our flight home
above clouds where there was snow on enough peaks in late July.

We were fortunate to have spent a year in Italy.

I will always remember
our day around the Dolomites,
with Giuseppe and his son Lorenzo,
whenever flying over the Alps.

The Alps were behind us now.

In the 1880s, in black and white photos,
Vittorio Sella documented the Dolomites,
Marmolada snow-covered in August 1891
and three figures with walking sticks
heading towards the peak or back
and how fragile they seemed,
not unlike the Iceman
who gave in to
snow and ice
more than
5,000 years ago
inside a gully which
preserved him until
global warming.

We saw Marmolada
from Passo Giau 2,000 meters above the sea,
and through binoculars, I followed the snow on top.
White. Fresh. From the night before.
The shadows grew by the end of the day
extending their reach across the mountainscape,
changing their forms as the wind kneaded the clouds,
what the Dolomites could not do in thousands of years but
did over time leaving fossils of sea things at their peaks.

In the fields,
there were cemeteries
with gardens next to churches
among the pines climbing the hills.

And so, the day went,
360 kilometers in 14 hours
up 6 Alpine passes around the Dolomites
from Bassano to the center of Cortina and
around the Gruppo di Sella with Marmolada in the distance
and back through the Valsugana Valley.

I had veal and red wine
and little of Nancy's fish but not her prosecco,
not bad for what you get on a plane.
The dark chocolate was good.
Nancy had picked it up at the airport
and gave most of it to me
while she made an anagram
out of *chocolate.*

Like Sand Castles

Moments are transitory,
yet they persist in our memories
even as they begin to fade
or become something else.

Like sand castles
eroding in the tide.

Leaving
before the last tower falls
holds the illusion
that they ever existed.

Notes

The inspiration for this work is simply Italy, where I handwrote lyrical impressions while Nancy painted oils on canvas during her 2001/02 sabbatical year in Bassano del Grappa. Since then, the material evolved to include several poems I wrote in recent years. In addition, the collection complements my creative nonfiction piece "Like a Polaroid Transfer," published in *The Account: A Journal of Poetry, Prose, and Thought.*

"Bastia Hill:" Dante Alighieri wrote about a small hill in a land between the Brenta and Piave rivers in *Paradiso* (Canto IX, 25–30). He also wrote about a tyrant who was born there in his *Inferno* (Canto XII, 109–10). The intersection of the two intrigued me.

"Homo Sapiens:" In 2001, I attended the *Plateau of Humankind,* the 49th exhibition of the Venice Biennale, which illustrated the state of the human race. The exhibit, curated by Harald Szeemann, caused me to reflect and reinterpret what I had experienced.

"Without Care:" Not long ago, I heard William Shatner, a Canadian actor who played James T. Kirk in the original *Star Trek* series, reflect on his experience in space on the Blue Origin space shuttle (October 2021). His feelings of "overwhelming sadness" surprised me; then inspired me to write this poem.

"Padre Pio:" Renzo Allegri, an Italian journalist, wrote *Padre Pio. L'uomo della speranza* (Arnoldo Mondadori Editore, 1984), and *I miracoli di Padre Pio* (Arnoldo Mondadori Editore, 1993). These books prompted me to write this piece within the context of 9/11.

"Coca Hotel:" In August 2007, inside an Italian church in Taormina, while Nancy was taking a pinhole photo, Liza Minnelli and her companion stepped in and asked where to make a donation. I pointed to the location without interrupting their visit. That evening, we saw Liza perform at an ancient theatre.

About the Author

R.G. Pagano lives in Newton, Massachusetts. He resided in Italy for a time and frequently travels there with his wife, drawing on those experiences for his creative work.

His poems have appeared in *Harrow House Journal, Lunch Ticket,* and Italian anthologies *Nei Miei Occhi, Tu* and *Ho Girato il Mondo per Incontrarti* (each associated with the Premio San Valentino–Atripalda, Italy).

His lyrical sensibility also extends to his short fiction in *SQUID Online Journal* and *Thirteen Bridges Review*; creative nonfiction in *The Account: A Journal of Poetry, Prose, and Thought*; and forthcoming novella, *Like Magic* (Type Eighteen Books, 2027).

Burnt Fields Under Snow is his first collection of poems.

www.ingramcontent.com/pod-product-compliance
Lightning Source LLC
LaVergne TN
LVHW090617110826
845146LV00001B/430

* 9 7 9 8 9 0 1 4 6 9 0 1 9 *